101 More Things To Do With A Cake Mix

101 Things MORE To Do With A Cake Mix

BY STEPHANIE ASHCRAFT

Gibbs Smith, Publisher
Salt Lake City

First Edition
08 07 06 05 04   5 4 3 2 1

Text © 2004 Stephanie Ashcraft

Published by
Gibbs Smith, Publisher
P.O. Box 667
Layton, Utah 84041

Orders: 1.800.748.5439
www.gibbs-smith.com

Edited by Suzanne Gibbs Taylor
Designed and produced by Kurt Wahlner
Printed and bound in Korea

Library of Congress Cataloging-in-Publication Data

Ashcraft, Stephanie.
101 more things to do with a cake mix / Stephanie Ashcraft.—1st ed.
       p. cm.
ISBN 1-58685-278-7
1. Cake. I. Title: One hundred one more things to do with a cake mix.
II. Title: One hundred and one more things to do with a cake mix.
III. Title.
   TX771.A816 2004
   641.8'653—dc22
                              2003018441

DEDICATION

To my husband and children,
who are my life and joy. And to
my mom—thanks for all the
help and advice.

Thank you to all my taste-testers
for your support, encouragement,
and feedback. You helped to
make this book possible.

CONTENTS

Cakes

Apple Spice Cake 60 • Berry Delight Cake 61 • Peaches-and-Cream Cake 62 • Pineapple Coconut Cake 63 • Pineapple Flop Cake 64 • Blueberry Swirl Cake 65 • Red, White and Blue Poke Cake 66 • Raspberry Poke Cake 67 • Exotic Carrot Cake 68 • Mom's Pineapple Carrot Cake 69 • Zucchini Nut Cake 70 • Peanut Butter Chocolate Chip Cake 71 • Strawberry Delight Cake 72

Bundt Cakes

Vanilla Spice Cake 74 • Cherry Swirl Cake 75 • Banana Pudding Cake 76 • Red Raspberry Dream Cake 77 • Blueberry Bundt Cake 78 • Spiced Apple Bundt Cake 79 • Sweet Strawberry Cream Cake 80 • Lemon Pie Cake 81 • Pumpkin Caramel Cake 82

Ice Cream Sandwiches and Cakes

Strawberry Ripple Ice Cream Sandwiches 84 • Tangy Ice Cream Sandwiches 85 • Banana Split Ice Cream Cake 86 • Butter Pecan Ice Cream Cake 87 • Peanut Butter Ice Cream Cake 88 • Strawberry Ice Cream Cake 89

Children's Delights

Apple Spice Cupcakes 92 • Boysenberry Delight Cupcakes 93 • Caramel Surprise Cupcakes 94 • Carrot Spice Cupcakes 95 • Cream-Filled Cupcakes 96 • Quick Pumpkin Cupcakes 97 • Peanut M&M Cake 98 • Raspberry Lemon Trifle 99 • Cherry Cheesecake Trifle 100 • Patriotic Trifle 101

Family-Favorite Desserts

Apple Dump Cake 104 • Cherry Peach Cobbler 105 • Sparkling Dump Cake 106 • Peanut Butter Lush 107 • Banana Pie Bars 108 • Cream Cheese Coconut Delight 109 • Chilled Cherry Pineapple Bars 110 • Peaches-and-Cream Pudding Bars 111 • Strawberry Lovers Parfaits 112 • Chewy Peanut Bars 113 • Pumpkin Crunch 114

Cheesecake and Dessert Pizzas

Pumpkin Cheesecake 116 • Raspberry Cheesecake Bars 117 • Blackberry Cheesecake Pudding Bars 118 • Decadent Chocolate Chip Cheesecake Bars 119 • Fruit Pizza 120 • Peanut Butter Lovers Pizza 121 • Peanut Butter Caramel-Apple Pizza 122 • Banana Split Pizza 123 • Rocky Road Pizza 124

HELPFUL HINTS

 Always beat cake batter with an electric mixer for at least 2 minutes.

 Always grease and flour the cake pan, or spray it with oil—even when the recipe doesn't call for it.

 Bake cakes on the middle oven rack, never on the top or bottom racks.

 For chewier cookies and bars, take them out of the oven just as they begin to turn golden brown around the edges and let them cool on or in the pan.

 For recipes using gelatin, make sure the gelatin is completely dissolved in hot water before adding any cold water.

 When using fresh fruit, dip it in pineapple, orange, or lemon juice so it won't change color.

 To see if a cake is done, insert a toothpick into the center—if it comes out clean, it's done. If the cake springs back when touched, that also means it's done.

 The first time you try a recipe, check the cake five minutes before its minimum cooking time ends—each oven heats differently.

 For best results, use glass or stoneware baking dishes.

 Don't overbake anything, especially cookies and bars. Finished products should always be moist and chewy.

BREAKFAST
SENSATIONS

EASY CINNAMON ROLLS

Rolls:

2 $1/4$ cups	**very warm water**
1 envelope (0.25 ounces)	
or 2 $1/4$ teaspoons	**active dry yeast**
1	**yellow** or **white cake mix**
5 cups	**flour**

Filling:

$1/2$ cup	**butter** or **margarine,** softened
1 cup	**brown sugar,** firmly packed
2 teaspoons	**cinnamon**
$1/4$ cup	**chopped nuts,** optional
$1/4$ cup	**raisins,** optional
1 can (16 ounces)	**cream cheese frosting**

Mix water and yeast together with a whisk in a large bowl. Whisk cake mix into yeast water. Stir in flour one cup at a time. Let dough stand in bowl in a draft-free place 45 minutes. Knead enough to punch down and roll to an 18 x 10-inch rectangle. Add small amount of flour if needed during process.

Mix butter, brown sugar, and cinnamon together. Heat in microwave 15 seconds. Spread over rolled-out dough. Sprinkle nuts or raisins over brown sugar mixture if desired. Starting with widest end, roll dough into a tight log. Cut into 15 rolls and place in a greased 9 x 13-inch pan. Allow rolls to rise 25 minutes. Bake at 350 degrees 19–23 minutes. Warm the cream cheese frosting in microwave 30–40 seconds. Drizzle desired amount of frosting over baked rolls. Makes 15 cinnamon rolls.

ORANGE ROLLS

Rolls:

2 $1/4$ cups	**very warm water**
I envelope (0.25 ounces)	
or 2 $1/4$ teaspoons	**active dry yeast**
I	**yellow** or **white cake mix**
I tablespoon	**grated orange rind**
5 cups	**flour**

Filling:

8 ounces	**cream cheese,** softened
$1/2$ cup	**sugar**
I $1/2$ tablespoons	**grated orange rind**

Frosting:

I cup	**powdered sugar**
2 tablespoons	**orange juice**

Mix water and yeast together with a whisk in a large bowl. Whisk cake mix into yeast water. Mix in orange rind. Stir in flour one cup at a time. Let dough stand in bowl in a draft-free place 45 minutes. Knead enough to punch down and roll to an 18 x 10-inch rectangle. Add small amount of flour if needed during process.

Mix cream cheese, sugar, and orange rind together. Spread over rolled-out dough. Starting with widest end, roll dough into a tight log. Cut into 15 rolls and place in a greased 9 x 13-inch pan. Allow rolls to rise 25 minutes. Bake at 350 degrees 19–23 minutes.

Mix powdered sugar and orange juice together until smooth. Spread over warm rolls. Makes 15 orange rolls.

STICKY BUNS

Buns:

2 1/4 cups	**very warm water**
I envelope (0.25 ounces) or 2 1/4 teaspoons	**active dry yeast**
I	**yellow** or **white cake mix**
5 cups	**flour**

Filling:

2 tablespoons	**butter** or **margarine,** softened
1/2 cup	**sugar**
2 teaspoons	**cinnamon**

Glaze:

1/2 cup	**butter** or **margarine,** melted
1/2 cup	**brown sugar,** firmly packed
2/3 cup	**chopped nuts,** optional
1/3 cup	**raisins,** optional

Mix water and yeast together with a whisk in a large bowl. Whisk cake mix into yeast water. Stir in flour one cup at a time. Let dough stand in bowl in a draft-free place 45 minutes. Knead enough to punch down and roll to an 18 x 10-inch rectangle. Add small amount of flour if needed during process.

Spread 2 tablespoons butter over rolled-out dough with pastry brush. Sprinkle sugar then cinnamon evenly over dough. Roll up dough beginning at widest end. Cut dough into 15 rolls.

Pour 1/2 cup melted butter into a 9 x 13-inch pan. Sprinkle brown sugar evenly over butter. Evenly distribute nuts and raisins over brown sugar, if desired. Place rolls in pan on brown sugar mixture. Let dough rise 25 minutes. Bake at 350 degrees 19–23 minutes. Invert hot rolls onto a platter. Makes 15 sticky buns.

BLUEBERRY APPLESAUCE MUFFINS

1	**white cake mix**
1 small box	**cheesecake** or **vanilla instant pudding**
3/4 cup	**water**
3	**eggs,** beaten
1/2 cup	**applesauce**
1 can (15 ounces)	**blueberries,** rinsed and drained

Preheat oven to 350 degrees. Lightly grease cups of muffin pan and set aside. Mix cake mix, pudding mix, water, eggs, and applesauce together until smooth. Stir in blueberries. Fill muffin cups 3/4 full. Bake 19–25 minutes or until light golden brown on top. Makes 24 muffins.

SWEET BANANA BREAD

1	**spice cake mix**
3	**large bananas,** mashed
3	**eggs**
1/2 cup	**finely chopped nuts** or **raisins,** optional

Preheat oven to 350 degrees. Mix all ingredients together until smooth. Divide batter between two greased bread pans. Bake 30 minutes or until a toothpick inserted into top of bread comes out clean.

BRUNCH CRUMB CAKE

Cake:

1 **yellow cake mix**
ingredients called for on back of box

Topping:

1/2 cup	**sugar**
1/2 cup	**brown sugar,** firmly packed
1 1/2 tablespoons	**cinnamon**
2 cups	**flour**
3/4 cup	**butter** or **margarine,** melted

Preheat oven to 350 degrees. Make cake batter as directed on back of box. Pour into a lightly greased-and-floured jelly roll pan or cookie sheet. Bake 15 minutes. Remove cake from oven and set aside.

Mix together all topping ingredients until crumbly. Sprinkle crumbs over top of cake. Bake an additional 10–15 minutes or until done.

APPLE COFFEE CAKE

Cake:

1	**yellow cake mix,** divided
1 cup	**flour**
1 envelope (0.25 ounces) or 2 1/4 teaspoons	**active dry yeast**
2/3 cup	**warm water**
2	**large eggs**
1 can (21 ounces)	**apple pie filling**
1/3 cup	**butter** or **margarine**

Glaze:

1 cup	**powdered sugar**
1 tablespoon	**milk**

Preheat oven to 350 degrees. Mix together 1 1/2 cups cake mix, flour, and yeast in a bowl. Add warm water, stirring until smooth. Stir in eggs. Spread batter evenly into a greased 9 x 13-inch pan. Spoon pie filling evenly over batter. In separate bowl, cut butter into remaining cake mix with fork until crumbly. Sprinkle mixture over pie filling. Bake 25–30 minutes or until light golden brown on top. Allow cake to cool.

Combine powdered sugar and milk. Drizzle over cake.

TRUE LOVE COFFEE CAKE

Cake:

I cup	**milk**
I envelope (0.25 ounces)	
or 2 $^1/_4$ teaspoons	**active dry yeast**
I	**yellow** or **white cake mix**
3	**eggs**
$^1/_2$ cup	**vegetable oil**
$^1/_2$ cup	**applesauce**

Topping:

$^3/_4$ cup	**brown sugar,** firmly packed
$^1/_2$ cup	**flour**
$^1/_4$ cup	**butter** or **margarine,** softened

Preheat oven to 350 degrees. Warm milk in microwave 35–45 seconds. Mix yeast with warm milk. Stir in cake mix. Mix in eggs, oil, and applesauce. Let stand in draft free place 5–10 minutes. Pour into a greased 9 x 13-inch pan and set aside.

In separate bowl, mix together brown sugar, flour, and butter until crumbly. Sprinkle topping over batter. Bake 25–35 minutes.

Cookies

AUNT IMOGENE'S
BUTTER PECAN COOKIES

1 **yellow** or **white cake mix**
2 **eggs**
$1/2$ cup **butter** or **margarine,** melted
1 can (16 ounces) **coconut pecan frosting**

Preheat oven to 350 degrees. With a spoon, mix cake mix, eggs, butter, and coconut pecan frosting together. Refrigerate dough 2 hours. Drop dough balls onto a lightly greased cookie sheet. Bake 10–11 minutes or until light golden brown around edges. Remove cookies and place on nonstick rack to cool.

BANANA NUT COOKIES

I	**white, yellow,** or **spice cake mix**
2	**eggs**
1/3 cup	**butter** or **margarine,** melted
1/3 cup	**applesauce**
I	**large banana,** mashed
3/4 cup	**chopped walnuts** or **pecans**

Preheat oven to 350 degrees. With a spoon, mix cake mix, eggs, butter, and applesauce together. Stir in banana and nuts. Drop dough balls onto a lightly greased cookie sheet. Bake 9–12 minutes or until light golden brown around edges. Remove cookies and place on nonstick rack to cool.

BUTTERSCOTCH PECAN COOKIES

1	**yellow** or **white cake mix**
1 small box	**butterscotch instant pudding**
1/2 cup	**flour**
2	**eggs**
1/2 cup	**vegetable oil** or **melted butter**
1 cup	**chopped pecans**

Preheat oven to 350 degrees. With a spoon, mix cake mix, pudding mix, flour, eggs, and oil or melted butter together. Stir in pecans. Drop dough balls onto an ungreased cookie sheet. Bake 9–12 minutes or until light golden brown around edges. Remove cookies and place on nonstick rack to cool.

BUTTERSCOTCH CHIP COOKIES

1 **white** or **yellow cake mix**
2 **eggs**
1/3 cup **vegetable oil** or **melted butter**
1 cup **butterscotch chips**

Preheat oven to 350 degrees. With a spoon, mix cake mix, eggs, and oil or melted butter together. Stir in butterscotch chips. Drop dough balls onto an ungreased cookie sheet. Bake 9–12 minutes or until light golden brown around edges. Remove cookies and place on nonstick rack to cool.

Peanut butter chips can be substituted for butterscotch chips and chocolate cake mix can be used in place of a white or yellow cake mix. If using chocolate cake mix, use 1/2 cup vegetable oil or melted butter.

CHOCOLATE CHIP CRUNCH COOKIES

$2/3$ cup	**butter-flavored shortening**
$1/2$ cup	**brown sugar,** firmly packed
2	**eggs**
1	**yellow** or **white cake mix**
1 cup	**crispy rice cereal**
1 cup	**semisweet** or **milk chocolate chips**
$1/2$ cup	**chopped walnuts** or **pecans**

Preheat oven to 350 degrees. With a fork, blend shortening and brown sugar together then stir in eggs one at a time. With a spoon, mix in cake mix. Stir in rice cereal, chocolate chips, and nuts. Drop dough balls onto a lightly greased cookie sheet. Bake 9–12 minutes or until light golden brown around edges. Do not overbake. Cool 2–3 minutes on cookie sheet. Remove cookies and place on nonstick rack to cool.

OATMEAL CHOCONUT COOKIES

1	**yellow** or **white cake mix**
2	**eggs**
1/2 cup	**butter** or **margarine,** softened
1/2 cup	**coconut**
1 1/2 cups	**quick oats**
1 cup	**milk chocolate chips**

Preheat oven to 350 degrees. With a spoon, mix cake mix, eggs, and butter together. Stir in coconut, oats, and chocolate chips. Drop dough balls onto a lightly greased cookie sheet. Bake 9–12 minutes or until light golden brown around edges. Remove cookies and place on non-stick rack to cool.

Semisweet chocolate or peanut butter chips can be used in place of milk chocolate chips.

MOIST OATMEAL RAISIN COOKIES

1	**spice cake mix**
2	**eggs**
1/3 cup	**vegetable oil**
1/3 cup	**applesauce**
2 cups	**quick oats**
1 cup	**raisins**

Preheat oven to 350 degrees. With a spoon, mix cake mix, eggs, oil, and applesauce together. Stir in oats and raisins. Drop dough balls onto a lightly greased cookie sheet. Bake 9–12 minutes or until light golden brown around edges. Remove cookies and place on nonstick rack to cool.

BUTTERSCOTCH CHIP OATMEAL COOKIES

1	**yellow** or **spice cake mix**
2	**eggs**
1/3 cup	**vegetable oil**
1/3 cup	**applesauce**
2 cups	**quick oats**
1 cup	**butterscotch chips**

Preheat oven to 350 degrees. With a spoon, mix cake mix, eggs, oil, and applesauce together. Stir in quick oats one cup at a time. Add butterscotch chips. Drop dough balls onto a lightly greased cookie sheet. Bake 9–12 minutes or until light golden brown around edges. Remove cookies and place on nonstick rack to cool.

CHERRY CHIP
SANDWICH COOKIES

1	**cherry chip cake mix**
2	**eggs**
1/3 cup	**vegetable oil**

1 can (16 ounces) **cherry** or **vanilla frosting**

Preheat oven to 350 degrees. With a spoon, mix cake mix, eggs, and oil together in large bowl. Drop 1-inch dough balls onto a greased cookie sheet. Bake 8–11 minutes or until light golden brown around edges. Remove cookies and place on nonstick rack to cool. Frost bottom of one cookie. Place another cookie on top to form sandwich. Makes 16–18 sandwich cookies.

Ice cream sandwiches can be made using this recipe by replacing frosting with a scoop of vanilla ice cream. Wrap sandwiches in plastic wrap and store in an airtight container in freezer.

CHEWY STRAWBERRY COOKIES

1	**strawberry cake mix**
2	**eggs**
2 cups	**whipped topping**
	powdered sugar

With a spoon, mix cake mix, eggs, and whipped topping together in large bowl. Refrigerate dough 2 hours. Preheat oven to 350 degrees. Roll 1-inch dough balls in powdered sugar, then drop onto a greased cookie sheet. Bake 6–9 minutes or until light golden brown around edges. Remove cookies and place on nonstick rack to cool. Store in refrigerator.

Makes a great sandwich cookie by adding frosting between two cookies.

WHITE CHOCOLATE CHIP LEMON COOKIES

1	**lemon cake mix**
2	**eggs**
1/3 cup	**vegetable oil**
1 cup	**white chocolate chips**

Preheat oven to 350 degrees. With a spoon, mix cake mix, eggs, and oil together. Stir in white chocolate chips. Drop dough balls onto a lightly greased cookie sheet. Bake 8–12 minutes or until light golden brown around edges. Remove cookies and place on nonstick rack to cool.

You can also do this recipe as bars in a 9 x 13-inch pan. Spread dough evenly into a lightly greased cake pan. Bake 14–16 minutes or until light golden brown around edges. Cool, then cut into bars.

ORANGE COOKIES

Cookies:

I	**white cake mix**
2	**eggs**
$^1/_4$ cup	**vegetable oil**
I cup	**flour**
$^1/_3$ cup	**orange juice**
I tablespoon	**finely grated orange peel**

Frosting:

2 tablespoons	**butter** or **margarine,** melted
I $^1/_2$ cups	**powdered sugar**
I $^1/_2$ teaspoons	**finely grated orange peel**
I–I $^1/_2$ tablespoons	**orange juice**

Preheat oven to 350 degrees. With a spoon, mix cake mix, eggs, oil, flour, and orange juice together. Stir in orange peel. Drop dough balls onto a lightly greased cookie sheet. Bake 10–13 minutes or until light golden brown around edges. Remove cookies and place on nonstick rack to cool.

Mix butter, powdered sugar, orange peel, and orange juice together. Frost individual cookies as desired.

PEANUT BUTTER CHOCOLATE CHIP COOKIES

2 **eggs**
1/3 cup **butter** or **margarine,** softened
1/2 cup **chunky peanut butter**
1 **yellow** or **white cake mix**
1 cup **chocolate chips** or **chunks**

Preheat oven to 350 degrees. With a spoon, mix eggs, butter, and peanut butter together. Stir in cake mix and then add chocolate. Drop dough balls onto a lightly greased cookie sheet. Bake 8–12 minutes or until light golden brown around edges. Remove cookies and place on non-stick rack to cool.

PEANUT BUTTER SANDWICH COOKIES

Cookies:

2	**eggs**
1/3 cup	**butter** or **margarine,** softened
1/2 cup	**chunky peanut butter**
1	**yellow** or **white cake mix**

Frosting:

1/4 cup	**butter** or **margarine,** melted
3 cups	**powdered sugar**
1 teaspoon	**vanilla**
2 tablespoons	**water**

Preheat oven to 350 degrees. With a spoon, mix eggs, butter, and peanut butter together. Stir in cake mix. Drop 1-inch dough balls onto a lightly greased cookie sheet. Bake 8–12 minutes or until light golden brown around edges. Remove cookies and place on nonstick rack to cool.

Mix butter, powdered sugar, vanilla, and water together until smooth. Spread frosting between two cooled cookies. Makes 16–18 sandwich cookies.

Ice cream sandwiches can be made using this recipe by replacing frosting with a scoop of vanilla or chocolate ice cream.

BUTTERSCOTCH CHIP PUMPKIN COOKIES

2	**packages yellow** or **spice cake mix**
I can (29 ounces)	**pumpkin**
2 cups	**butterscotch chips***

Preheat oven to 350 degrees. With a spoon, stir cake mixes and pumpkin together in a large bowl. Stir in butterscotch chips. Drop by rounded spoonfuls onto a lightly greased cookie sheet. Bake 8–12 minutes. Cool 2–3 minutes on cookie sheet before removing to a nonstick rack to cool completely.

Do not double this recipe.

*Milk chocolate chips can be substituted for butterscotch chips.

SPICED PUMPKIN NUT COOKIES

1	**spice cake mix**
1 can (15 ounces)	**pumpkin**
1/2 cup	**chopped nuts**
1 cup	**milk chocolate chips** or **raisins,** optional

Preheat oven to 350 degrees. With a spoon, mix cake mix and pumpkin together in large bowl. Stir in nuts and, if desired, chocolate chips or raisins. Drop by rounded spoonfuls onto a lightly greased cookie sheet. Bake 8–12 minutes. Cool 2–3 minutes on cookie sheet before removing to a nonstick rack to cool completely.

WHITE CHOCOLATE CHUNK COOKIES

I	**yellow** or **white cake mix**
2	**eggs**
$^1/_2$ cup	**butter** or **margarine,** softened
I cup	**rolled oats**
$^1/_2$ cup	**chopped pecans**
$^3/_4$ cup	**coconut**
2	**white chocolate candy bars, cut into $^1/_4$- to $^1/_2$-inch chunks**

Preheat oven to 350 degrees. With a spoon, mix cake mix, eggs, and butter together. Stir in rolled oats, pecans, coconut, and white chocolate. Drop dough balls onto an ungreased cookie sheet. Bake 8–12 minutes or until light golden brown around edges. Remove cookies and place on nonstick rack to cool.

One cup semisweet or milk chocolate chips can be substituted for white chocolate. For a lower-fat version, $^1/_4$ cup applesauce and $^1/_3$ cup vegetable oil can be substituted for $^1/_2$ cup butter.

MACADAMIA NUT COOKIES

1	**white** or **yellow cake mix**
2	**eggs**
1/3 cup	**vegetable oil**
1 cup	**white chocolate chips** or **chunks**
1/2 cup	**chopped macadamia nuts**

Preheat oven to 350 degrees. With a spoon, mix cake mix, eggs, and oil together. Stir in white chocolate and nuts. Drop dough balls onto an ungreased cookie sheet. Bake 8–12 minutes or until light golden brown around edges. Remove cookies and place on nonstick rack to cool.

One cup semisweet or milk chocolate chips or chunks can be substituted in place of white chocolate.

ANDES MINTS SURPRISE COOKIES

1 **white** or **yellow cake mix**
2 **eggs**
¹/₃ cup **vegetable oil**
30–36 individual **Andes mints,** unwrapped

Heat oven to 350 degrees. With a spoon, mix cake mix, eggs, and oil together in a bowl. Flatten a ball of dough around a chocolate mint. Make sure candy is completely covered with dough. Bake 8–12 minutes or until light golden brown around edges. Remove cookies and place on nonstick rack to cool.

A chocolate cake mix can be used, but increase vegetable oil from ¹/₃ cup to ¹/₂ cup.

Brownies and Bars

CARAMEL CASHEW BARS

Bars:

I	**yellow** or **white cake mix**
2	**eggs**
1/3 cup	**vegetable oil** or **melted butter**
I cup	**chopped cashews**
I cup	**semisweet** or **milk chocolate chips**

Topping:

25	**caramels,** unwrapped
1/8 cup	**milk**

Preheat oven to 350 degrees. With a spoon, mix cake mix, eggs, and oil or melted butter together. Stir in cashews and chocolate chips. Spread dough evenly into a lightly greased 9 x 13-inch pan. Bake 16–20 minutes or until light golden brown around edges.

In saucepan, thoroughly melt caramels and milk together, stirring constantly. Pour caramel topping evenly over baked dessert. Cool completely and cut into bars.

CARAMEL CHOCOLATE SURPRISE BARS

1	**yellow cake mix**
1/2 cup	**butter** or **margarine,** melted
1/4 cup	**evaporated milk**
1 cup	**chocolate chips**
3/4 cup	**chopped nuts**
1 jar (12 ounces)	**caramel ice cream topping**

Preheat oven to 350 degrees. With a spoon, mix cake mix, butter, and evaporated milk together. Spread 3/4 of dough evenly into a greased 9 x 13-inch pan. Spread chocolate chips and nuts over bottom layer. Pour caramel topping evenly over top. Break rest of dough into small pieces and drop evenly over top. Bake 20–25 minutes. Cool 30 minutes. Cut into bars. Store in refrigerator.

FALL HARVEST BARS

1	**yellow** or **white cake mix**
2	**eggs**
1/3 cup	**vegetable oil** or **melted butter**
1/2 cup	**Skor toffee bits** or **crushed Butterfinger bars**
1/2 cup	**chocolate chips**

Preheat oven to 350 degrees. With a spoon, mix cake mix, eggs, and oil or melted butter together. Stir in candy and chocolate chips. Spread dough evenly into a lightly greased 9 x 13-inch pan. Bake 14–20 minutes or until light golden brown around edges. Cut into bars and serve warm or at room temperature.

HEAVENLY CHIP BARS

1	**yellow** or **white cake mix**
1/2 cup	**butter** or **margarine,** melted
1	**egg**
1/2 cup	**creamy peanut butter**
1 can (14 ounces)	**sweetened condensed milk**
1 cup	**chocolate chips**
1 cup	**peanut butter chips**
3/4 cup	**chopped nuts,** optional

Preheat oven to 350 degrees. With a spoon, mix cake mix, butter, egg, and peanut butter together. Press dough into a lightly greased 9 x 13-inch pan. Pour sweetened condensed milk over dough layer. Sprinkle top evenly with chocolate chips, peanut butter chips, and nuts if desired. Bake 20–25 minutes or until light golden brown around edges. Cool completely and cut into bars.

COOKIE-DOUGH BLONDIES

Bottom Layer:
1	**yellow** or **white cake mix**
1/2 cup	**butter** or **margarine,** softened
1	**egg**
1 teaspoon	**vanilla**
1/4 cup	**brown sugar,** firmly packed
3/4 cup	**semisweet chocolate chips**

Filling:
1/2 cup	**butter** or **margarine,** softened
1/2 cup	**brown sugar**
1/4 cup	**sugar**
2 tablespoons	**milk**
1 teaspoon	**vanilla**
1 cup	**flour**

Frosting:
1 tablespoon	**butter** or **margarine**
1 cup	**semisweet chocolate chips**

Preheat oven to 350 degrees. With a spoon, mix cake mix, butter, egg, vanilla, and brown sugar together. Stir in chocolate chips. Spread evenly into a greased 9 x 13-inch pan. Bake 15–20 minutes or until light golden brown around edges. Do not overbake. Cool completely.

In a separate bowl, mix 1/2 cup butter, brown sugar, and sugar together. Stir in milk and vanilla. Mix in flour. Spread evenly over cooled bottom layer.

Melt tablespoon of butter and 1 cup of chocolate chips together in a small saucepan until smooth. Spread melted chocolate over top. Cut into bars and refrigerate at least 2 hours. Store in refrigerator.

PEANUT BUTTER CRUNCH BARS

Bars:

1	**white** or **yellow cake mix**
2	**eggs**
1/3 cup	**vegetable oil**
1/2 cup	**creamy peanut butter**

Topping:

1 cup	**semisweet** or **milk chocolate chips**
1/2 cup	**creamy peanut butter**
1 1/2 cups	**crispy rice cereal**

Preheat oven to 350 degrees. With a spoon, mix cake mix, eggs, and oil together. Stir in peanut butter. Spread dough evenly into a lightly greased 9 x 13-inch pan. Bake 14–18 minutes or until light golden brown around edges. Set aside.

In saucepan, melt chocolate chips and peanut butter together over low heat. Remove from heat. Fold crispy rice cereal into melted chocolate sauce. Spread mixture evenly over dessert. Cool completely and chill at least 2 hours. Cut into bars before serving. Store in refrigerator.

HEAVENLY WHITE BROWNIES

1	**white cake mix**
1/2 cup	**butter** or **margarine,** melted
1	**egg**
3/4 cup	**chopped pecans**
3/4 cup	**coconut**
8 ounces	**cream cheese,** softened
1/2 teaspoon	**vanilla**
2	**eggs**
1-pound box	**powdered sugar**

Preheat oven to 350 degrees. With a spoon, mix cake mix, butter, and egg together. Press dough into a lightly greased 9 x 13-inch pan. Sprinkle pecans and coconut evenly over top.

In a separate bowl, gradually beat cream cheese, vanilla, and eggs together with an electric mixer. Slowly beat in powdered sugar. Spread cream cheese mixture evenly over top. Bake 30–35 minutes or until light golden brown around edges. Store in refrigerator.

PEANUT BUTTER CHOCOLATE DELIGHTS

Bars:

1	**yellow cake mix**
¹/₂ cup	**butter** or **margarine,** melted
1	**egg**
1 ¹/₂ cups	**coconut**
1 can (14 ounces)	**sweetened condensed milk**

Topping:

1 ¹/₂ cups	**semisweet** or **milk chocolate chips**
¹/₃ cup	**creamy peanut butter**

Preheat oven to 350 degrees. With a spoon, mix cake mix, butter, and egg together. Press dough into bottom of a lightly greased 9 x 13-inch glass pan. Sprinkle coconut over top. Pour sweetened condensed milk evenly over coconut. Bake 20–25 minutes or until light golden brown around edges.

Melt chocolate chips and peanut butter together in a saucepan over low heat. Spread chocolate over hot coconut layer. Cool 30 minutes. Chill at least 2 hours. Store in refrigerator.

PEANUT BUTTER M&M BARS

1	**white** or **yellow cake mix**
2	**eggs**
1/3 cup	**vegetable oil**
1/2 cup	**crunchy peanut butter**
1–1 1/2 cups	**M&Ms**

Preheat oven to 350 degrees. With a spoon, mix cake mix, eggs, oil, and peanut butter together in large bowl. Mix M&Ms into dough. Press into a lightly greased 9 x 13-inch pan. Bake 14–18 minutes or until light golden brown around edges. Cool 15–20 minutes before cutting into bars.

MINT CHIP BARS

1	**white** or **yellow cake mix**
2	**eggs**
1/3 cup	**vegetable oil**
1 cup	**mint chips**

Preheat oven to 350 degrees. With a spoon, mix cake mix, eggs, and oil together. Stir in mint chips. Spread dough evenly into a lightly greased 9 x 13-inch pan. Bake 14–16 minutes. Cool, then cut into bars.

For cookies, drop dough balls onto a lightly greased cookie sheet. Bake 8–10 minutes. Remove cookies and place on nonstick rack to cool.

A chocolate cake mix can be used instead, just increase vegetable oil from 1/3 cup to 1/2 cup.

EASY LAYER BARS

Bottom Layer:
- 1 **yellow cake mix**
- $^1/_2$ cup **butter** or **margarine,** melted
- 1 **egg**

Top Layer:
- 1 can (14 ounces) **sweetened condensed milk**
- 1 cup **coconut**
- 1 cup **chocolate chips**
- 1 cup **butterscotch chips**
- $^3/_4$ cup **chopped nuts**

Preheat oven to 350 degrees. With a spoon, mix cake mix, butter, and egg together. Press dough into a lightly greased 9 x 13-inch pan. Pour sweetened condensed milk over dough layer. Sprinkle coconut, chocolate chips, butterscotch chips, and nuts evenly over top. Bake 20–25 minutes or until light golden brown around edges. Cool completely and cut into bars.

OATMEAL CARAMEL-APPLE BARS

Bars:

1	**yellow, white,** or **spice cake mix**
2	**eggs**
1/2 cup	**butter** or **margarine,** softened
1 1/2 cups	**rolled oats**
2 cups	**chopped apples**
1/2 cup	**chopped walnuts** or **pecans**

Topping:

1/2 cup	**flour**
1 jar (16 ounces)	**caramel ice cream topping**

Preheat oven to 350 degrees. With a spoon, mix cake mix, eggs, and butter together. Stir in rolled oats. Press into a greased 9 x 13-inch pan. Sprinkle apples and nuts evenly over dough. Bake 25–30 minutes.

In saucepan, mix flour and caramel topping. Stirring constantly, bring to boil. Continue stirring and boil 3–5 minutes to thicken. Remove from heat and drizzle caramel topping over dessert. Cool completely. Refrigerate for an hour and cut into bars. Store in an airtight container in refrigerator.

STRAWBERRY PUDDING BARS

Bars:
1	**strawberry cake mix**
2	**eggs**
1/3 cup	**vegetable oil**
1 cup	**white chocolate** or **vanilla chips**

Topping:
1 small box	**vanilla** or **cheesecake instant pudding**
1 1/2 cups	**milk**

Preheat oven to 350 degrees. With a spoon, mix cake mix, eggs, and oil together. Stir in white chips. Spread dough evenly into a lightly greased 9 x 13-inch pan. Bake 14–18 minutes or until light golden brown around edges. Immediately poke holes in dessert at 1-inch intervals with a wooden spoon handle.

Beat pudding mix and milk together 2 minutes with wire whisk. Pour half of pudding over warm dessert. Let rest of pudding chill and thicken 5–10 minutes. Frost with remaining pudding. Cut into bars and store in refrigerator.

LUSCIOUS LEMON BARS

Bars:

1	**white** or **yellow cake mix**
1/2 cup	**butter** or **margarine,** melted
1	**egg**

Filling:

3	**eggs,** slightly beaten
1 3/4 cups	**sugar**
1/4 cup	**flour**
1 teaspoon	**baking powder**
1/4 cup	**lemon juice**
	powdered sugar, to garnish

Preheat oven to 350 degrees. With a spoon, mix cake mix, butter, and egg together. Press into a greased 9 x 13-inch pan. Mix eggs, sugar, flour, baking powder, and lemon juice together. Spread evenly over dough. Bake 30–35 minutes or until light golden brown on top. Cool completely. Sprinkle powdered sugar over top and cut into bars. Store in refrigerator.

PINEAPPLE DREAM BARS

Bars:

1	**white** or **yellow cake mix**
1/2 cup	**butter** or **margarine**, melted
1	**egg**

Filling:

8 ounces	**cream cheese,** softened
2 tablespoons	**sugar**
2 tablespoons	**milk**
1 teaspoon	**vanilla**
1	**egg**
1 can (8 ounces)	**crushed pineapple,** drained
1–1 1/2 cups	**coconut**

Glaze:

3/4 cup	**powdered sugar**
1/4 teaspoon	**vanilla**
3–4 teaspoons	**milk**

Preheat oven to 350 degrees. With a spoon, mix cake mix, butter, and egg together. Press into a lightly greased 9 x 13-inch pan.

Beat cream cheese, sugar, milk, vanilla, and egg together in a separate bowl until smooth. Stir in well-drained pineapple. Spread evenly over dough. Sprinkle coconut over top. Bake 25–30 minutes or until coconut is light golden brown. Cool completely.

Mix powdered sugar, vanilla, and milk together in a small bowl. Drizzle glaze evenly over cooled dessert. Refrigerate at least 2 hours and cut into bars. Store in refrigerator.

BUTTER PECAN BARS

Bars:

1	**butter pecan** or **white cake mix**
2	**eggs**
1/3 cup	**butter** or **margarine,** melted
1 teaspoon	**vanilla**
1/2 cup	**chopped pecans**

Frosting:

2 tablespoons	**butter** or **margarine,** melted
2 cups	**powdered sugar**
1/4 teaspoon	**vanilla**
2–3 tablespoons	**milk**

24–30	**pecan halves,** optional

Preheat oven to 350 degrees. With a spoon, mix cake mix, eggs, butter, and vanilla together. Stir in pecans. Press dough into a lightly greased 9 x 13-inch pan. Bake 14–16 minutes or until light golden brown around edges. Cool 15–20 minutes.

Mix butter, powdered sugar, vanilla, and milk to make frosting. Spread evenly over top of cooled dessert. Cut into bars. Place a pecan half in the center of each bar if desired.

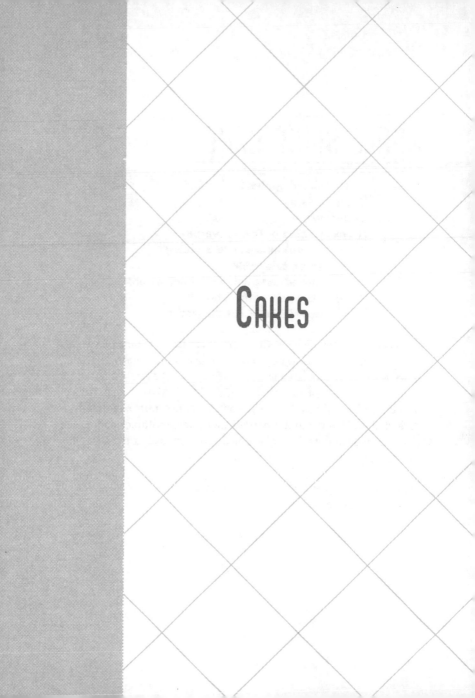

CAKES

APPLE SPICE CAKE

3 cups	**sliced apples**
1/2 cup	**raisins**
1/2 cup	**water**
I small box	**vanilla** or **French vanilla**
	cook-and-serve pudding*
I	**spice cake mix**
	ingredients listed on back of box
1/2 cup	**chopped nuts,** optional
	powdered sugar, to garnish

Preheat oven to 350 degrees. Cut apple slices into bite-size pieces. Mix together apples, raisins, water, and pudding mix in a microwave-safe bowl. Microwave on high 4 minutes. Stir and spread apple mixture evenly over bottom of a greased 9 x 13-inch pan. Make cake batter as directed on back of box. Pour over apples. Sprinkle nuts over top if desired. Bake 30–40 minutes or until an inserted toothpick comes out clean. Cool 20 minutes. Sprinkle powdered sugar over top. Serve with vanilla ice cream or whipped topping.

Try butterscotch pudding with a white cake mix in place of vanilla pudding and spice cake mix.

*Do not use instant pudding in this recipe.

BERRY DELIGHT CAKE

Cake:

1	**white** or **vanilla cake mix**
3	**eggs**
1/2 cup	**sour cream**
3/4 cup	**water**
1/2 cup	**applesauce**
1 can (15 ounces)	**blueberries** or **blackberries,** drained and rinsed

Topping:

8 ounces	**whipped topping**
8 ounces	**blueberry** or **blackberry yogurt**

Preheat oven to 350 degrees. Mix cake mix, eggs, sour cream, water, and applesauce together 2 minutes until smooth. Gently fold in berries with a spatula. Pour batter into a greased-and-floured 9 x 13-inch pan. Bake 25–30 minutes or until an inserted toothpick comes out clean. Allow cake to cool completely. Cover and refrigerate 2–3 hours.

Before serving, gently stir whipped topping and yogurt together, then frost cake. Store in refrigerator.

PEACHES-AND-CREAM CAKE

1	**white cake mix**
1 small box	**peach gelatin**
2	**eggs**
1 1/4 cups	**juice from drained peaches**
	and/or **water**
1/3 cup	**vegetable oil**
1 can (29 ounces)	**sliced peaches,** drained and divided
12 ounces	**whipped topping**

Preheat oven to 350 degrees. Beat cake mix, gelatin, eggs, juice, and oil together 1–2 minutes on low speed with electric mixer. Cut peach slices into chunks, enough to measure 1 1/4 cups. Mix peach chunks into batter. Pour batter into a greased 9 x 13-inch pan. Bake 30–35 minutes or until an inserted toothpick comes out clean. Allow cake to cool. Cover and refrigerate 2–3 hours.

Before serving, spread whipped topping over cake. Arrange leftover peach slices over top. Store in refrigerator.

PINEAPPLE COCONUT CAKE

Cake:

1	**white** or **yellow cake mix**
4	**eggs**
1 can (20 ounces)	**crushed pineapple,** with juice
1/2 cup	**vegetable oil**
1 cup	**coconut**

Topping:

12 ounces	**whipped topping**
1 can (8 ounces)	**crushed pineapple,** with juice
1 small box	**coconut cream instant pudding**
1 cup	**coconut**

Preheat oven to 350 degrees. Mix cake mix, eggs, pineapple with juice, and oil together in a large bowl. Stir in 1 cup coconut. Bake in a greased 9 x 13-inch pan 30–35 minutes or until an inserted toothpick comes out clean. Chill at least 2 hours.

Before serving, mix together whipped topping, pineapple with juice, and pudding mix until smooth. Spread over cake. Sprinkle 1 cup coconut over top. Store in refrigerator.

PINEAPPLE FLOP CAKE

$1/2$ cup	**butter** or **margarine**
$3/4$ cup	**brown sugar,** firmly packed
I can (20 ounces)	**pineapple slices,** reserve juice
I small jar	**maraschino cherries,** drained and halved
I	**yellow** or **white cake mix**
	ingredients listed on back of box

Preheat oven to 350 degrees. Melt butter in a 9 x 13-inch pan. Sprinkle brown sugar evenly in pan. Place pineapple slices over brown sugar in a regular pattern. Place cherry halves in the middle of each pineapple ring. Make cake batter as directed on back of box. (Drained pineapple juice can be used instead of water called for on box.) Pour batter over pineapple. Bake 35–45 minutes or until an inserted toothpick comes out clean. Let stand in pan 5 minutes. Invert hot cake onto a serving platter.

BLUEBERRY SWIRL CAKE

Cake:

1	**white cake mix**
1/3 cup	**oil**
2	**eggs**
3/4 cup	**water**
1 can (21 ounces)	**blueberry pie filling**

Frosting:

8 ounces	**cream cheese,** softened
1 cup	**powdered sugar**
12 ounces	**whipped topping**

Preheat oven to 350 degrees. Mix cake mix, oil, eggs, and water together. Stir in pie filling. Pour batter into a greased 9 x 13-inch pan. Bake 30–35 minutes or until an inserted toothpick comes out clean. Allow cake to cool.

Before serving, mix together cream cheese, powdered sugar, and whipped topping. Spread over cake. Store in refrigerator.

RED, WHITE AND BLUE POKE CAKE

1 **white cake mix**
ingredients called for on back of box

2 cups **milk**
1 small box **cheesecake** or **vanilla instant pudding**

1 can (21 ounces) **cherry pie filling**
1 can (21 ounces) **blueberry pie filling**
12 ounces **whipped topping**

Make cake batter as directed on back of box and pour into a greased 9 x 13-inch pan. Bake as directed and let cool. With handle of a wooden spoon, poke holes at 1-inch intervals clear through cake. Add milk to pudding mix and beat with wire whisk 2 minutes. Refrigerate pudding 5 minutes. Pour pudding over cake. Spread cherry pie filling over top and then blueberry pie filling over top of cherry. Cover with whipped topping. Refrigerate at least 2 hours before serving. Store in refrigerator.

RASPBERRY POKE CAKE

1	**white cake mix**
	ingredients listed on back of box
1 small box	**raspberry gelatin**
1 cup	**boiling water**
1/2 cup	**cold water**
8 ounces	**cream cheese,** softened
8 ounces	**whipped topping**
1 can (21 ounces)	**raspberry pie filling**

Make cake batter as directed on back of box and pour into a greased 9 x 13-inch pan. Bake as directed and let cool. Poke deep holes into cake with a fork, about 1 inch apart.

Dissolve gelatin in 1 cup boiling water. Then add cold water to gelatin. Slowly pour gelatin mixture into holes.

Mix together softened cream cheese and whipped topping. Spread over top of cake. Spoon pie filling evenly over top. Refrigerate at least 3 hours before serving. Store in refrigerator.

EXOTIC CARROT CAKE

1	**spice cake mix**
3	**eggs**
1/3 cup	**vegetable oil**
1 1/4 cups	**water**
1 cup	**shredded carrot**
1/2 cup	**chopped walnuts**
1/2 cup	**coconut**
1 cup	**chocolate chips** or **raisins,** optional
1 can (16 ounces)	**cream cheese frosting**

Preheat oven to 350 degrees. Beat cake mix, eggs, oil, water, and shredded carrot together 2 minutes with electric mixer at low speed. Mix nuts, coconut, and chocolate chips or raisins if desired into cake batter. Pour batter into a greased-and-floured 9 x 13-inch pan. Bake 27–35 minutes or until an inserted toothpick comes out clean. Remove cake from oven and cool 15–20 minutes. Spread cream cheese frosting over top.

MOM'S PINEAPPLE CARROT CAKE

1	**carrot cake mix**
6	**egg whites**
1 can (20 ounces)	**crushed pineapple,** with juice
$^1/_2$ cup	**olive oil**
$^1/_2$ cup	**grated** or **chopped nuts**
1 can (16 ounces)	**cream cheese frosting** or **powdered sugar,** to garnish

Preheat oven to 350 degrees. Beat cake mix, egg whites, pineapple with juice, and olive oil together. Stir in nuts. Pour batter into a greased 9 x 13-inch pan. Bake 28–35 minutes or until an inserted toothpick comes out clean. Remove cake from oven and cool 15–20 minutes. Frost cake with cream cheese frosting or sprinkle powdered sugar over top.

ZUCCHINI NUT CAKE

        1   **yellow cake mix**
        3   **eggs**
 1/4 cup   **vegetable oil**
 1/4 cup   **applesauce**
 1/2 cup   **water**
 2 1/2 to 3 **small zucchini,** peeled and grated*
 3/4 cup   **raisins** or **mini chocolate chips**
 1/2 cup   **chopped walnuts**

1 can (16 ounces)   **cream cheese frosting** or
                    powdered sugar, to garnish

Preheat oven to 350 degrees. Beat cake mix, eggs, oil, applesauce, and water together. Stir in zucchini, raisins or chocolate chips, and nuts. Pour batter into a greased-and-floured 9 x 13-inch pan. Bake 28–33 minutes or until an inserted toothpick comes out clean. Frost cake with cream cheese frosting or sprinkle powdered sugar over top.

*If using large zucchini, remove seeds before grating. Use approximately 2 cups grated zucchini.

PEANUT BUTTER CHOCOLATE CHIP CAKE

Cake:

1	**white cake mix**
	ingredients called for on back of box
1/2 cup	**chunky peanut butter**
1 cup	**chocolate chips**

Frosting:

1 can (16 ounces)	**white frosting**
1/4 cup	**creamy peanut butter**
1/2 cup	**chopped nuts,** optional

Preheat oven to 350 degrees. Make cake batter as directed on back of box. Mix in peanut butter with electric mixer. Stir in chocolate chips. Pour batter into a greased 9 x 13-inch pan. Bake 25–30 minutes or until an inserted toothpick comes out clean. Allow cake to cool completely.

Mix frosting and peanut butter together. Spread over top of cooled cake. Sprinkle with nuts if desired.

STRAWBERRY DELIGHT CAKE

I	**strawberry cake mix**
	ingredients called for on back of box
I cup	**white chocolate** or **vanilla chips**
I large box	**vanilla** or **cheesecake instant pudding**
8 ounces	**whipped topping**
	sliced strawberries, optional

Preheat oven to 350 degrees. Mix cake batter as directed on back of box with electric mixer 2 minutes. Stir in white chips. Pour batter into a greased 9 x 13-inch pan. Bake as directed. Allow cake to cool.

While cake is cooling, make instant pudding according to directions on box. Allow pudding to thicken in refrigerator. Cut cake into long, skinny pieces. Place one slice of cake on a small plate. Place a large scoop of pudding over cake. Place another slice of cake over pudding. Add more pudding. Top with whipped topping. If desired, garnish each serving with sliced strawberries.

BUNOT CAKES

VANILLA SPICE CAKE

³/₄ cup	**sour cream**
4	**eggs**
¹/₂ cup	**water**
¹/₂ cup	**oil**
1	**spice cake mix**
1 small box	**vanilla instant pudding**
	powdered sugar, to garnish

Preheat oven to 350 degrees. Beat sour cream, eggs, water, and oil together in a large bowl. Add cake mix and pudding mix. Pour batter into a greased-and-floured tube or bundt pan. Bake 45–50 minutes or until an inserted toothpick comes out clean. Invert hot cake onto a platter. When cool, sift powdered sugar over cake.

CHERRY SWIRL CAKE

1 **white cake mix**
3 **eggs**
2 cans (21 ounces) **cherry pie filling,** divided

8 ounces **whipped topping**

Preheat oven to 350 degrees. Mix cake mix and eggs together. Stir in one can of pie filling. Pour batter into a greased tube or bundt cake pan. Bake 40–50 minutes or until an inserted toothpick comes out clean. Invert hot cake onto a platter. Serve individual pieces with reserved pie filling and whipped topping.

BANANA PUDDING CAKE

1 1/2 cups **milk**
1 small box **banana instant pudding**
1 **spice cake mix**
1/3 cup **vegetable oil**
3 **eggs**
2 **bananas,** mashed

1 can (16 ounces) **white frosting** or
powdered sugar, to garnish

Preheat oven to 350 degrees. Mix milk and pudding together until pudding stiffens. Mix cake mix, oil, and eggs into pudding. Stir in bananas. Pour batter into a greased tube or bundt cake pan. Bake 45–50 minutes or until an inserted toothpick comes out clean. Invert hot cake onto a platter. When cake has cooled, spread white frosting or sift powdered sugar over cake.

RED RASPBERRY DREAM CAKE

1 **white cake mix**
3 **eggs**
1 can (21 ounces) **raspberry pie filling**

8 ounces **whipped topping**
$^1/_2$ **white chocolate bar,** grated
$^1/_2$ cup **chopped** or **grated nuts**

Preheat oven to 350 degrees. Mix cake mix and eggs together. Stir in pie filling. Pour batter into a greased tube or bundt cake pan. Bake 40–50 minutes or until an inserted toothpick comes out clean. Invert hot cake onto a platter. Serve individual pieces with a scoop of whipped topping. Sprinkle grated chocolate and nuts over top.

BLUEBERRY BUNDT CAKE

1	**white cake mix**
3	**eggs**
1 can (21 ounces)	**blueberry pie filling**
8 ounces	**whipped topping**

Preheat oven to 350 degrees. Mix cake mix and eggs together. Stir in pie filling. Pour batter into a greased tube or bundt cake pan. Bake 40–50 minutes or until an inserted toothpick comes out clean. Invert hot cake onto a platter. Serve individual pieces with a scoop of whipped topping or vanilla ice cream.

SPICED APPLE BUNDT CAKE

I	**spice cake mix**
3	**eggs**
I can (21 ounces)	**apple pie filling**

caramel ice cream topping, or
powdered sugar, to garnish

Preheat oven to 350 degrees. Mix cake mix and eggs together. Stir in pie filling. Pour batter into a greased tube or bundt cake pan. Bake 40–50 minutes or until an inserted toothpick comes out clean. Invert hot cake onto a platter. When cool, drizzle caramel topping or sift powdered sugar over top.

SWEET STRAWBERRY CREAM CAKE

³/₄ cup	**sour cream**
4	**eggs**
¹/₂ cup	**water**
¹/₂ cup	**oil**
1	**strawberry cake mix**
1 small box	**cheesecake** or **vanilla instant pudding**
1 cup	**white chocolate** or **vanilla chips**
	powdered sugar, to garnish
	whipped topping
	strawberries, sliced

Preheat oven to 350 degrees. Beat sour cream, eggs, water, and oil together. Add cake mix and pudding mix. Stir in white chips. Place batter in a greased-and-floured tube or bundt cake pan. Bake 45–50 minutes or until an inserted toothpick comes out clean. Invert hot cake onto a platter. When cool, sift powdered sugar on top of cake. Serve each individual piece with whipped topping and sliced straw berries over top.

LEMON PIE CAKE

1	**white** or **lemon cake mix**
3	**eggs**
1 can (15 ounces)	**lemon pie filling**
1 can (16 ounces)	**white frosting** or
	powdered sugar, to garnish

Preheat oven to 350 degrees. Mix cake mix and eggs together. Stir in pie filling. Pour batter into a greased tube or bundt cake pan. Bake 45–50 minutes or until an inserted toothpick comes out clean. Invert hot cake onto a platter. When cool, spread white frosting or sift powdered sugar over top.

PUMPKIN CARAMEL CAKE

1	**spice** or **butter pecan cake mix**
¹/₄ cup	**applesauce**
2	**eggs**
1 can (15 ounces)	**pumpkin**
1 jar (12 ounces)	**caramel ice cream topping**
	whipped topping

Preheat oven to 350 degrees. Mix cake mix, applesauce, and eggs together. Stir in pumpkin. Pour batter into a greased tube or bundt cake pan. Bake 38–45 minutes or until an inserted toothpick comes out clean. Invert hot cake onto a platter. Drizzle each individual piece of cake with caramel topping and a dollop of whipped topping before serving.

ICE CREAM
SANDWICHES
AND CAKES

STRAWBERRY RIPPLE
ICE CREAM SANDWICHES

1 **strawberry cake mix**
1/3 cup **oil**
2 **eggs**

1/2 gallon **strawberry ripple ice cream**

Preheat oven to 350 degrees. With a spoon, mix cake mix, oil, and eggs together. Drop 1-inch dough balls onto an ungreased cookie sheet. Bake 8–12 minutes or until light golden brown around edges. Leave cookies on cookie sheet 2–3 minutes. Remove cookies and place on nonstick rack to cool.

Once cooled, place a scoop of ice cream between two cookies. Wrap sandwiches in plastic wrap. Store in an airtight container in freezer. Makes 16–18 ice cream sandwiches.

TANGY ICE CREAM SANDWICHES

1	**lemon** or **orange cake mix**
1/3 cup	**vegetable oil**
2	**eggs**
1/2 gallon	**vanilla ice cream**

Preheat oven to 350 degrees. With a spoon, mix cake mix, oil, and eggs together. Drop 1-inch dough balls onto an ungreased cookie sheet. Bake 8–12 minutes or until light golden brown around edges. Leave cookies on cookie sheet 2–3 minutes. Remove cookies and place on nonstick rack to cool.

Once cooled, place a scoop of ice cream between two cookies. Wrap sandwiches in plastic wrap. Store in an airtight container in freezer. Makes 16–18 ice cream sandwiches.

BANANA SPLIT
ICE CREAM CAKE

1	**yellow** or **white cake mix**
1	**egg**
¹/₂ cup	**butter** or **margarine,** melted

2 boxes (¹/₂ gallon)	**vanilla, chocolate,** or **strawberry ice cream,** softened
1 jar (12 ounces)	**pineapple ice cream topping**
1 jar (12 ounces)	**strawberry** or **fudge ice cream topping**
³/₄ cup	**chopped nuts,** optional
2	**bananas,** sliced

Preheat oven to 350 degrees. With a spoon, mix cake mix, egg, and butter together. Press dough into a lightly greased 9 x 13-inch pan. Bake 7–10 minutes. Crust will not be cooked completely. Freeze 1 hour.

Spread 1 box of softened ice cream evenly over crust. Freeze 1 hour. Spread pineapple topping over ice cream. Spread second box of softened ice cream over pineapple. Freeze another 1–2 hours. Spread strawberry or fudge topping evenly over cake. Sprinkle nuts over top, if desired. Cover and freeze at least 3 hours or overnight. Serve with freshly sliced bananas. Store in freezer.

Two different flavors of ice cream can be used.

BUTTER PECAN
ICE CREAM CAKE

1	**yellow, white,** or **butter pecan cake mix**
1	**egg**
1/2 cup	**butter** or **margarine,** melted

2 boxes (1/2 gallon)	**butter pecan ice cream,** softened
1 jar (12 ounces)	**butterscotch** or **caramel**
	ice cream topping
3/4 cup	**chopped pecans**

Preheat oven to 350 degrees. With a spoon, mix cake mix, egg, and butter together. Press dough into a lightly greased 9 x 13-inch pan. Bake 7–10 minutes. Crust will not be cooked completely. Cool.

Spread both boxes of ice cream over crust. Spread topping over ice cream layer. Sprinkle pecans over top. Cover and freeze 4 hours or overnight. Store in freezer.

PEANUT BUTTER
ICE CREAM CAKE

I	**yellow** or **white cake mix**
I	**egg**
$^1/_2$ cup	**butter** or **margarine,** melted
2 boxes ($^1/_2$ gallon)	**vanilla** or **chocolate** **ice cream,** softened
$^2/_3$ cup	**peanut butter**
I cup	**corn syrup**
$^3/_4$ cup	**chopped nuts**

Preheat oven to 350 degrees. With a spoon, mix cake mix, egg, and butter together. Press dough into a lightly greased 9 x 13-inch pan. Bake 7–10 minutes. Crust will not be cooked completely. Cool.

Spread both boxes of ice cream over crust. Soften peanut butter in microwave-safe bowl 10–30 seconds on high. Stir in corn syrup. Spread peanut butter topping over ice cream layer. Sprinkle nuts on top. Cover and freeze at least 4 hours before serving. Store in freezer.

STRAWBERRY ICE CREAM CAKE

1	**yellow, white,** or **strawberry cake mix**
1	**egg**
$^1/_2$ cup	**butter** or **margarine,** melted
2 boxes ($^1/_2$ gallon)	**strawberry, strawberry ripple,** or **strawberry cheesecake ice cream,** softened
1 jar (12 ounces)	**strawberry ice cream topping**
	sliced strawberries, optional

Preheat oven to 350 degrees. With a spoon, mix cake mix, egg, and butter together. Press dough into a lightly greased 9 x 13-inch pan. Bake 7–10 minutes. Crust will not be cooked completely. Cool.

Spread both boxes of ice cream over crust. Spread strawberry topping over top. Cover and freeze at least 4 hours before serving. Serve with freshly sliced strawberries if desired. Store in freezer.

CHILDREN'S DELIGHTS

APPLE SPICE CUPCAKES

I	**spice cake mix**
3	**eggs**
I ¹/₄ cups	**water**
¹/₃ cup	**applesauce**
I cup	**chopped apples**

I can (16 ounces)   **vanilla** or **cream cheese frosting**

Preheat oven to 350 degrees. Lightly grease cups of muffin pan and set aside. Mix cake mix, eggs, water, and applesauce together until smooth. Stir in apples. Fill muffin cups ²/₃ full and bake 18–23 minutes or until done. Remove cupcakes from pan to cool completely.

Top cupcakes with frosting. Makes 24 cupcakes.

BOYSENBERRY DELIGHT CUPCAKES

Cupcakes:
	1	**white cake mix**
		ingredients called for on back of box
	8 ounces	**boysenberry yogurt***

Frosting:
	8 ounces	**whipped topping**
	8 ounces	**boysenberry yogurt***

Preheat oven to 350 degrees. Lightly grease cups of muffin pan and set aside. Make cake batter as directed on back of box. Fold in yogurt. Fill muffin cups $^2/_3$ full and bake 18–23 minutes or until done. Chill cupcakes in refrigerator at least 3 hours.

Stir whipped topping and yogurt together. Frost cupcakes just before serving and enjoy. Store in refrigerator. Makes 24 cupcakes.

*Yogurt with fruit on the bottom yields best results. Blueberry, raspberry, or lemon yogurt can be used in place of boysenberry.

CARAMEL SURPRISE CUPCAKES

1 **yellow** or **white cake mix**
   ingredients listed on back of box
1 cup **butterscotch** or **chocolate chips**
24 **caramels,** unwrapped*

1 can (16 ounces) **chocolate** or **white frosting**

Preheat oven to 350 degrees. Lightly grease cups of muffin pan and set aside. Make cake batter as directed on back of box. Stir in butterscotch or chocolate chips. Fill muffin cups $^1/_3$ full and set unused batter aside. Bake 5 minutes. Place caramel in center of each cupcake. Top caramel with remaining cake batter to fill muffin cups $^2/_3$ full. Bake an additional 10–14 minutes or until done. Remove from pan and allow to cool completely.

Top cupcakes with frosting. Makes 24 cupcakes.

*Unwrapped miniature chocolate peanut butter cups or individual Rolos candies can be substituted in place of caramels.

CARROT SPICE CUPCAKES

1	**spice cake mix**
	ingredients listed on back of box
1 1/4 cups	**shredded carrot**
1/2 teaspoon	**cinnamon**
1/2 cup	**chopped** or **grated nuts**
1 can (16 ounce)	**white** or **cream cheese frosting**

Preheat oven to 350 degrees. Lightly grease cups of muffin pan and set aside. Make cake batter as directed on back of box. Stir in carrot, cinnamon, and nuts. Fill muffin cups 2/3 full. Bake 18–23 minutes or until done. Remove from pan and allow to cool completely.

Top cupcakes with frosting. Makes 24 cupcakes.

CREAM-FILLED CUPCAKES

Cupcakes:

> 1 **strawberry** or **lemon cake mix***
> **ingredients listed on back of box**

Filling:

> 8 ounces **cream cheese,** softened
> 1 **egg**
> 2 cups **powdered sugar**

> 1 can (16 ounces) **vanilla, white,** or **cream cheese frosting**

Preheat oven to 350 degrees. Line cups of muffin pan with cupcake liners and set aside. Make cake batter as directed on back of box. Fill muffin cups 1/2 full.

Mix cream cheese, egg, and powdered sugar together in a separate bowl. Place a tablespoon of cream cheese filling in center of each cupcake. Bake 18–23 minutes. Remove cupcakes from pan and cool completely.

Top cupcakes with frosting. Makes 24 cupcakes.

*Any flavor cake mix can be used for this recipe for endless possibilities.

QUICK PUMPKIN CUPCAKES

1	**spice cake mix**
2	**eggs**
1 cup	**pumpkin**
1/3 cup	**water**

1 can (16 ounces)	**cream cheese** or **white frosting**
	candy pumpkins, optional

Preheat oven to 350 degrees. Lightly grease cups of muffin pan and set aside. Mix cake mix, eggs, pumpkin, and water together. Fill muffin cups 2/3 full. Bake 15–20 minutes. Remove cooled cupcakes from pan.

Top cupcakes with frosting. If desired, place a candy pumpkin on top of frosted cupcake. Makes 24 cupcakes.

PEANUT M&M CAKE

1	**chocolate** or **yellow cake mix** **ingredients called for on back of box**
1/2 cup	**flour**
1 cup	**peanut M&Ms**
1 can (16 ounces)	**white frosting**
1/4 cup	**creamy peanut butter** **peanut M&Ms,** to garnish

Preheat oven to 350 degrees. Make cake batter as directed on back of box. Stir in flour and peanut M&Ms. Pour batter into a greased 9 x 13-inch pan. Bake 30–35 minutes or until an inserted toothpick comes out clean. Allow cake to cool completely.

Mix frosting and peanut butter together. Frost cake and place peanut M&Ms around outer edge to make a fun border.

RASPBERRY LEMON TRIFLE

1 **white cake mix**
ingredients listed on back of box

1 can (14 ounces) **sweetened condensed milk**
8 ounces **lemon yogurt**
1/3 cup **lemon juice**
1 1/2 teaspoons **grated lemon peel**
2 cups **whipped topping**

2 cups **raspberries***

Make cake batter as directed on back of box and pour into a 9 x 13-inch pan. Bake as directed.

Mix condensed milk, yogurt, lemon juice, and lemon peel together. Gently fold whipped topping into yogurt mixture.

Crumble half of cooled cake into bottom of punch bowl. Pour half of yogurt mixture over cake. Crumble other half of cake into bowl and pour remaining yogurt mixture over that. Garnish with raspberries. Store in refrigerator.

*Blueberries or strawberries can be used in place of raspberries.

CHERRY CHEESECAKE TRIFLE

1 **white cake mix**
ingredients listed on back of box

8 ounces **cream cheese,** softened
1 cup **sour cream**
$^1/_2$ cup **milk**
1 small box **vanilla** or **cheesecake instant pudding**
8 ounces **whipped topping**

2 cans (21 ounces) **cherry pie filling***

Make cake batter as directed on back of box and pour into a 9 x 13-inch pan. Bake as directed.

Mix cream cheese, sour cream, milk, and pudding mix together until smooth and thick. Gently fold whipped topping into cream cheese mixture.

Crumble half of cooled cake into bottom of punch bowl. Pour half of cream cheese mixture over cake crumbs. Spread one can of pie filling over cream cheese layer. Crumble other half of cake into bowl and pour rest of cream cheese mixture over that layer. Spread remaining pie filling over top. Store in refrigerator.

*Any flavor pie filling can be used in this recipe.

PATRIOTIC TRIFLE

1	**white cake mix**
	ingredients on back of box
2 small boxes	**vanilla** or **cheesecake instant pudding**
4 cups	**milk**
1 can (21 ounces)	**cherry pie filling**
1 can (21 ounces)	**blueberry pie filling**
12 ounces	**whipped topping**
1/2 cup	**chopped nuts**

Make cake batter as directed on back of box and pour into a 9 x 13-inch pan. Bake as directed.

Combine pudding mixes and milk 2 minutes with a wire whisk. Allow pudding to thicken in refrigerator 5 minutes or more.

Crumble half of cooled cake into bottom of punch bowl. Pour half of pudding over cake. Crumble other half of cake into bowl and pour remaining pudding over top. Spread blueberry pie filling over pudding, then cherry pie filling, then whipped topping. Sprinkle nuts over top. Store in refrigerator.

Family-Favorite Desserts

APPLE DUMP CAKE

1 **yellow cake mix**
1 can (21 ounces) **apple pie filling**
$^1/_3$–$^1/_2$ cup **butter** or **margarine,** melted

Preheat oven to 350 degrees. Grease a 9 x 13-inch pan. Dump half of cake mix evenly into bottom of pan. Spread pie filling evenly over cake mix. Cover with remaining cake mix. Drizzle butter over top. Do not mix. Bake 47–52 minutes or until light golden brown. Serve warm with a scoop of vanilla ice cream or whipped topping.

CHERRY PEACH COBBLER

1	**yellow cake mix**
1 can (21 ounces)	**cherry pie filling**
1 can (29 ounces)	**peach slices,** reserve juice

Preheat oven to 350 degrees. Grease a 9 x 13-inch pan. Dump half of cake mix evenly into bottom of pan. Spread pie filling evenly over cake mix. Drain juice from peaches into a separate container. Cover cherries with peach slices. Cover fruit layer with remaining cake mix. Pour peach juice over top. Do not mix. Bake 47–52 minutes or until light golden brown. Serve warm with a scoop of vanilla ice cream or whipped topping.

SPARKLING DUMP CAKE

I can (21 ounces)   **apple, cherry,** or **blueberry pie filling**
            I   **yellow** or **white cake mix**
I can (12 ounces)   **lemon-lime soft drink**

Preheat oven to 350 degrees. Pour pie filling in bottom of a lightly greased 9 x 13-inch pan. Pour dry cake mix over top of pie filling. Pour soft drink evenly over pie filling and cake mix. Do not mix. Bake 47–52 minutes or until light golden brown. Serve warm with a scoop of vanilla ice cream or whipped topping.

PEANUT BUTTER LUSH

Crust:

1	**white** or **yellow cake mix**
1/2 cup	**butter** or **margarine,** melted
1	**egg**

Pudding Layer:

2 small boxes	**chocolate instant pudding**
3 cups	**cold milk**

Peanut Butter Layer:

1/3 cup	**creamy peanut butter**
1/4 cup	**cold milk**
12 ounces	**whipped topping**

nuts, to garnish
chocolate syrup, to garnish

Preheat oven to 350 degrees. With a spoon, mix cake mix, butter, and egg together. Press dough into a lightly greased 9 x 13-inch pan. Bake 14–18 minutes or until light golden brown around edges. With a spoon, remove air pockets by pushing down evenly over entire hot crust. Allow crust to cool completely.

Beat pudding mixes and 3 cups cold milk with wire whisk 2 minutes. Spread evenly over cooled crust. In a separate bowl, mix peanut butter, 1/4 cup cold milk, and whipped topping together with wire whisk. Gently spread peanut butter layer evenly over pudding layer. Chill 3–4 hours before serving. To garnish, sprinkle nuts and drizzle chocolate syrup lightly over top before serving. Store in refrigerator.

BANANA PIE BARS

1 **white** or **yellow cake mix**
1/2 cup **butter** or **margarine,** melted
1 **egg**

2 **medium bananas,** thinly sliced
2 small boxes **banana instant pudding**
3 cups **cold milk**
12 ounces **whipped topping**

Preheat oven to 350 degrees. With a spoon, mix cake mix, butter, and egg together. Press dough into a lightly greased 9 x 13-inch pan. Bake 14–18 minutes or until light golden brown around edges. With a spoon, remove air pockets by pushing down evenly over entire hot crust. Allow crust to cool completely.

Place bananas evenly over crust. Beat pudding mixes and cold milk with wire whisk 2 minutes. Spread evenly over banana slices. Chill 3–4 hours, then spread whipped topping over top before serving. Store in refrigerator.

CREAM CHEESE COCONUT DELIGHT

1	**white** or **yellow cake mix**
1/2 cup	**butter** or **margarine,** melted
1	**egg**
8 ounces	**cream cheese,** softened
1/4 cup	**sugar**
2 tablespoons	**milk**
12 ounces	**whipped topping,** divided
2 small boxes	**coconut cream instant pudding**
3 cups	**milk**
1/2 cup	**coconut**

Preheat oven to 350 degrees. With a spoon, mix cake mix, butter, and egg together. Press dough into a lightly greased 9 x 13-inch pan. Bake 14–18 minutes or until light golden brown around edges. With a spoon, remove air pockets by pushing down evenly over entire hot crust. Allow crust to cool completely.

Beat cream cheese, sugar, and 2 tablespoons milk together. Gently stir in 1 cup (8 ounces) whipped topping. Spread over cooled crust. Beat pudding mixes and 3 cups milk together 2 minutes in a large bowl. Spread over cream cheese layer. Refrigerate 3–4 hours. Before serving, spread remaining whipped topping (4 ounces) over pudding layer. Sprinkle coconut over top. Store in refrigerator.

CHILLED CHERRY PINEAPPLE BARS

I	**white** or **yellow cake mix**
I	**egg**
$1/3-1/2$ cup	**butter** or **margarine,** melted
2 cans (21 ounces)	**cherry pie filling**
I can (20 ounces)	**crushed pineapple,** drained
12 ounces	**whipped topping**
I can (14 ounces)	**sweetened condensed milk**
I cup	**chopped pecans**

Preheat oven to 350 degrees. With a spoon, mix cake mix, egg, and butter together. Press dough into a lightly greased 9 x 13-inch pan. Bake 14–18 minutes or until light golden brown around edges. With a spoon, remove air pockets by pushing down evenly over entire hot crust. Allow crust to cool completely.

In a separate bowl, stir pie filling, pineapple, whipped topping, and sweetened condensed milk together. Pour over cooled crust. Sprinkle pecans over top. Refrigerate 4 or more hours. Store in refrigerator. Cut into bars and serve.

PEACHES-AND-CREAM PUDDING BARS

1	**white** or **yellow cake mix**
1	**egg**
1/3–1/2 cup	**butter** or **margarine,** melted
2 small boxes	**vanilla** or **cheesecake instant pudding**
3 cups	**milk**
1 can (29 ounces)	**sliced peaches,** drained
12 ounces	**whipped topping**
	fresh sliced peaches, optional

Preheat oven to 350 degrees. With a spoon, mix cake mix, egg, and butter together. Press dough into a lightly greased 9 x 13-inch pan. Bake 14–18 minutes or until light golden brown around edges. With a spoon, remove air pockets by pushing down evenly over entire hot crust. Allow crust to cool completely.

Mix together pudding mix and milk until thick. Chill pudding 5–10 minutes. Place half of sliced peaches evenly over top of cooled crust. Spread half of pudding over peaches. Place remaining peaches over pudding. Spread remaining pudding over peaches. Cover and chill at least 3 hours.

Before serving, frost dessert with whipped topping and garnish with fresh peaches if desired. Cut into bars and serve. Store in refrigerator.

STRAWBERRY LOVERS PARFAITS

Cookie Layer:
- 1 **strawberry cake mix**
- 2 **eggs**
- 1/2 cup **butter** or **margarine,** softened
- 1 cup **white chocolate chips**

Pudding Layer:
- 2 small boxes **vanilla instant pudding**
- 4 cups **milk**

Strawberry Layer:
- 12–16 ounces **whipped topping**
- **sliced strawberries,** optional

Preheat oven to 350 degrees. With a spoon, mix cake mix, eggs, and butter together. Stir in white chocolate chips. Press dough into a greased 9 x 13-inch pan. Bake 14–18 minutes or until light golden brown around edges. Allow to cool uncovered 1–2 hours.

Mix pudding mix and milk together. Chill 5 minutes. Crumble cookie layer into a separate bowl. In parfait glasses, layer cookie crumbs, pudding, whipped topping, and strawberries. Repeat for three layers. Makes 12 large parfaits.

CHEWY PEANUT BARS

1	**white cake mix**
1	**egg**
1/2 cup	**butter** or **margarine,** melted
3 1/2 cups	**miniature marshmallows**
1 3/4 cups	**peanut butter chips**
3 tablespoons	**butter** or **margarine**
2/3 cup	**corn syrup**
1 can (16 ounces)	**chopped peanuts**

Preheat oven to 350 degrees. With a spoon, mix cake mix, egg, and butter together. Press dough into a lightly greased 9 x 13-inch pan. Bake 15–18 minutes or until light golden brown around edges. With a spoon, remove air pockets by pushing down evenly over entire hot crust. Immediately sprinkle marshmallows evenly over top. Return pan to oven for an additional 2–3 minutes. Remove and allow to cool.

Melt peanut butter chips and 3 tablespoons butter in a small saucepan. Stir in corn syrup. Bring peanut butter chip mixture to a light boil, stirring occasionally. Remove pan from heat and pour mixture over marshmallow layer. Sprinkle peanuts evenly over top. Cool completely and cut into bars before serving.

PUMPKIN CRUNCH

4	**eggs**
1 cup	**sugar**
2 teaspoons	**pumpkin pie spice**
1 can	**evaporated milk**
1 teaspoon	**salt**
1 can (15 ounces)	**pumpkin**
1 box	**yellow** or **spice cake mix**
1/2 cup	**butter** or **margarine,** melted
1 cup	**chopped pecans** or **almonds**
8 ounces	**whipped topping**

Preheat oven to 350 degrees. Slightly beat eggs in a large bowl. Add sugar, pumpkin pie spice, evaporated milk, salt, and pumpkin into beaten eggs. Pour into a lightly greased 9 x 13-inch pan. Sprinkle cake mix evenly over pumpkin mixture. Drizzle butter over entire cake mix layer. Sprinkle nuts evenly over top. Bake 50 minutes. Allow to cool 1 hour. Refrigerate at least 2 hours. Serve each individual piece with a scoop of whipped topping. Store in refrigerator.

Cheesecake and Dessert Pizzas

PUMPKIN CHEESECAKE

Crust:

1	**spice cake mix**
1/2 cup	**butter** or **margarine,** melted
1	**egg**

Filling:

3 (8-ounce) packages	**cream cheese,** softened
1 cup	**sugar**
1 teaspoon	**vanilla**
1 can (15 ounces)	**pumpkin**
1 teaspoon	**cinnamon**
1/2 teaspoon	**nutmeg**
1/2 teaspoon	**allspice**
3	**eggs**

Preheat oven to 325 degrees. With a spoon, mix cake mix, butter, and egg together. Divide dough in half. Press dough into bottom of two lightly greased pie pans.

Mix together cream cheese, sugar, vanilla, pumpkin, and spices. Mix in each egg, one at a time. Pour half of filling over one crust. Pour remaining filling over other crust. Bake both cheesecakes 50–55 minutes or until center is firm. Store in refrigerator.

RASPBERRY CHEESECAKE BARS

Crust:

1	**white** or **yellow cake mix**
1/2 cup	**butter** or **margarine,** melted
1	**egg**
1 jar (12 ounces)	**seedless raspberry jam,** divided

Filling:

2 (8-ounce) packages	**cream cheese,** softened
3/4 cup	**sugar**
1/2 teaspoon	**vanilla**
1/2 teaspoon	**grated lemon peel**
3	**eggs**

Preheat oven to 350 degrees. With a spoon, mix cake mix, butter, and egg together. Spread dough into bottom of a greased 9 x 13-inch pan. Stir jam until smooth. Spread 3/4 cup (6 ounces) jam evenly over crust layer.

Mix cream cheese, sugar, vanilla, and lemon peel together. Beat in one egg at a time. Pour mixture over jam layer. Bake 25–35 minutes or until golden brown and center is firm. Allow cheesecake to cool.

In saucepan, heat remaining jam. Drizzle over cooled cheesecake. Refrigerate 3 hours or overnight. Store in refrigerator. Cut into bars before serving.

BLACKBERRY CHEESECAKE PUDDING BARS

Crust:
	1	**white cake mix**
	1/2 cup	**butter** or **margarine,** melted
	1	**egg**

Filling:
	8 ounces	**cream cheese,** softened
	1 cup	**powdered sugar**
	1 1/2 cups	**milk**
	1 small box	**cheesecake instant pudding**
	8 ounces	**whipped topping**
	1 can (21 ounces)	**blackberry pie filling***

Preheat oven to 350 degrees. With a spoon, mix cake mix, butter, and egg together. Press dough into a lightly greased 9 x 13-inch pan. Bake 14–18 minutes or until light golden brown around edges. With a spoon, remove air pockets by pushing down evenly over entire hot crust. Allow crust to cool completely.

Beat cream cheese and powdered sugar together. Gradually beat in milk and pudding mix until smooth. Allow mixture to thicken in refrigerator 5 minutes. Gently fold whipped topping into mixture with a spatula. Spread over cooled crust. Spoon pie filling evenly over top. Chill at least 2 hours before serving. Cut into bars before serving. Store in refrigerator.

*Use blueberry or cherry pie filling in place of blackberry filling.

DECADENT CHOCOLATE CHIP CHEESECAKE BARS

Cookie Layers:

1	**white cake mix**
1/2 cup	**flour**
2	**eggs**
1/3 cup	**vegetable oil**
3/4 cup	**chocolate chips**

Cream Cheese Layer:

4 ounces	**cream cheese,** softened
1/2 cup	**sugar**
1	**egg**

Preheat oven to 350 degrees. With a spoon, mix cake mix, flour, eggs, and oil together. Stir in chocolate chips. Press half of dough into a greased 8 x 8-inch pan.

In a separate bowl, mix cream cheese, sugar, and egg together until smooth. Spread cream cheese mixture over bottom layer. Crumble remaining cookie dough evenly over top. Bake 24–28 minutes or until light golden brown. Cool, then cut into bars. Store in refrigerator.

FRUIT PIZZA

1 **white cake mix**
1 **egg**
$^1/_2$ cup **butter** or **margarine,** melted
$^1/_2$ cup **flour**

$^1/_4$ cup **powdered sugar**
8 ounces **cream cheese,** softened
8 ounces **whipped topping**
**sliced strawberries, bananas, kiwi,
pineapple, apple, blueberries,
peaches,** or **grapes**
coconut, optional

Preheat oven to 350 degrees. With a spoon, mix cake mix, egg, and butter together. Mix in flour. Spread dough thinly to cover a lightly greased jelly roll pan or cookie sheet. Bake 10–14 minutes or until light golden brown around edges. Allow to cool completely.

Mix powdered sugar, cream cheese, and whipped topping together. Spread over cookie layer. Top with sliced fruit of choice. Sprinkle coconut over top if desired. Store in refrigerator.

PEANUT BUTTER LOVERS PIZZA

I	**yellow** or **chocolate cake mix**
I	**egg**
1/2 cup	**butter** or **margarine,** melted
1/2 cup	**flour**
I small box	**vanilla** or **chocolate instant pudding**
I 1/2 cups	**milk**
1/2 cup	**plain yogurt**
1/3 cup	**peanut butter**
3 small	**Butterfinger bars,** chopped*

Preheat oven to 350 degrees. With a spoon, mix cake mix, egg, and butter together. Mix in flour. Spread dough thinly to cover a lightly greased jelly roll pan or cookie sheet. Bake 10–14 minutes or until light golden brown around edges. Allow to cool completely.

Beat pudding mix, milk, yogurt, and peanut butter together. Refrigerate at least 5–10 minutes. Before serving, spread mixture over top of cooled cookie layer. Sprinkle candy over top.

*Use crushed chocolate peanut butter cups, M&Ms, or Reese's Pieces in place of Butterfinger bars.

PEANUT BUTTER CARAMEL-APPLE PIZZA

	1	**white cake mix**
1	**egg**
1/2 cup	**butter** or **margarine,** melted
1/2 cup	**flour**

8 ounces	**cream cheese,** softened
1/2 cup	**brown sugar,** firmly packed
1/4 cup	**creamy peanut butter**
1/2 teaspoon	**vanilla**
1 1/2 cups	**chopped apples***

| 1/3 cup | **caramel ice cream topping** |
| 3/4 cup | **chopped peanuts,** unsalted |

Preheat oven to 350 degrees. With a spoon, mix cake mix, egg, and butter together. Mix in flour. Spread dough thinly to cover a lightly greased jelly roll pan or cookie sheet. Bake 10–14 minutes or until light golden brown around edges. Allow to cool completely.

Mix together cream cheese, brown sugar, peanut butter, and vanilla. Spread evenly over top of cooled cookie. Arrange apple pieces over cream cheese mixture.

Warm caramel topping in a microwave-safe dish 30-45 seconds. Drizzle over apples. Sprinkle nuts over pizza. Store in refrigerator.

*Dip apple pieces in lemon juice or lemon-lime soda to prevent them from turning brown.

BANANA SPLIT PIZZA

I	**white** or **vanilla cake mix**
I	**egg**
¹/₂ cup	**butter** or **margarine,** melted
¹/₂ cup	**flour**
¹/₄ cup	**powdered sugar**
8 ounces	**cream cheese,** softened
8 ounces	**whipped topping**
I can (8 ounces)	**pineapple chunks,** drained
2	**bananas,** thinly sliced
I ¹/₂ cups	**strawberries,** sliced
¹/₂ cup	**chopped nuts**
	caramel ice cream topping, optional

Preheat oven to 350 degrees. With a spoon, mix cake mix, egg, and butter together. Mix in flour. Spread dough thinly to cover a lightly greased jelly roll pan or cookie sheet. Bake 10–14 minutes or until light golden brown around edges. Allow to cool completely.

Mix powdered sugar, cream cheese, and whipped topping together. Spread over cookie layer. Top evenly with fruit and nuts. Drizzle caramel topping over top if desired. Store in refrigerator.

ROCKY ROAD PIZZA

1	**chocolate cake mix**
1	**egg**
1/2 cup	**butter** or **margarine,** melted

2 cups	**miniature marshmallows**
1 1/2 cups	**milk chocolate chips**
3/4 cup	**chopped nuts**
1/2 cup	**caramel ice cream topping**

Preheat oven to 350 degrees. With a spoon, mix cake mix, egg, and butter together. Spread dough thinly to cover a lightly greased jelly roll pan or cookie sheet. Bake 10 minutes. Top hot crust evenly with marshmallows, chocolate chips, and nuts. Drizzle caramel topping over pizza. Return to oven for an additional 3–5 minutes to puff marshmallows and slightly melt chocolate. Cool 10 minutes before serving.

ABOUT THE AUTHOR

Stephanie Ashcraft, author of *101 Things To Do With A Cake Mix* and *101 Things To Do With A Slow Cooker,* was raised near Kirklin, Indiana. She received a bachelor's degree in family science and a teaching certificate from Brigham Young University. Stephanie loves teaching, interacting with people, and spending time with friends and family. Since 1998, she has taught cooking classes throughout the state of Utah. She and her husband, Ivan, reside in Provo with their children. Being a mom is her full-time job.

101 THINGS TO DO WITH A CAKE MIX and
101 THINGS TO DO WITH A SLOW COOKER
BY STEPHANIE ASHCRAFT

Each: 128 pages, $9.95

Available at bookstores
or directly from GIBBS SMITH, PUBLISHER
1.800.748.5439